MW00891894

Dad Jokes

Jokes So Bad, They Are Funny

George Smith

Table of Contents

© Copyright 2018 - All rights reserved.

It is not legal to reproduce, duplicate, or transmit any part of this document in either electronic means or in printed format. Recording of this publication is strictly prohibited.

Introduction

I would like to congratulate you for buying this book, but since you have exposed yourself to the literary equivalent of gastro enteritis it would be in bad taste, rather like the pages you are about to read.

It would be irresponsible not to offer a health warning as well. Some of the jokes you will come across, over the next several thousand words, are so bad that they could induce any of the following conditions:

Headache

Breathlessness

Stomach Pain

Aching Sides

Involuntary contractions of the airways

Watering eyes

Running nose

Lost voice

Loud guffaw sounds emanating from your mouth…in fact, the symptoms of…

Joking **to death.**

Indeed, it is possible that some of the readers of this collection of, frankly, awful jokes will need hospitalization to get themselves back on an even keel. In fact, you would be ***ill***-advised (and trust me, as jokes go, that is one of the better ones) to read this alone, or at least without arranging for a friend to check on you in a couple of hours.

In these days of gender fluidity, the idea of jokes being constrained to being told by just dads is rather old fashioned – not as old as some of the gags you are about to read, but then, nothing living today could be – and so I am very happy for them to be read and told by men, women, wives, mothers, fathers, children, dogs and slugs, a creature at the intellectual level needed to fully appreciate the wit, word play, irony and satire of jokes of the quality of, for example:

Why did Cyclops give up teaching?

Because he only had *one pupil.*

Please, feel free to take a rest and gather yourself together before continuing.

Indeed, thinking about teaching reminds me of the English teacher who asked the science teacher out on a date.

He read her poetry throughout their romantic meal, but, why not? After all, that's

What he *met-a-phor*

Good one, eh? Bet it made you *simile.*

Back to this wonderful book. A few words about the author, George Smith. George is one of the funniest men on the planet. At least, that's what his wife says. But she puts it better. *'Odd'* is the synonym she uses. In fact, she often adds the word 'worryingly' in front of the adjective. But their private life is their business.

This book will make you a healthier, saner, more rounded person. OK, so maybe your job is on the line, your partner's joined the gym and has bought a load of new clothes, and had a tattoo with 'I Love My New Boyfriend' on her arm (I know that doesn't work if you are her new boyfriend, but you're not going to get perfection for the money you paid for this book), your kids have entered adolescent grunt land, your car will cost more to repair than it is worth, the roof's leaking and Donald Trump is President. But read just one of the jokes that follow, and you will realize how bad life could really become.

So, read on and delight. As you will know, 'delight' means *turn to dark.* A darkened room is what you'll need after recovering from the hundreds of jokes in this book.

And when you've finished, spread the laughter. Buy some glue, cut up the pages and stick them on strangers. That way, the *jokes on them.*

Chapter One: Vampires, Zombies And Other Creatures From The Dark

In this chapter you will learn about the mysterious world of creatures from the underworld, the living dead and the dead unliving. You will learn that their favorite drink is any kind of *spirit* (they turn to *Sprite* when hungover or dyslexic) and that every one of them keeps a bowl of fruit in their sitting room. A bowl full of *blood oranges* and *neck-tarines.*

You will learn how vampires *cloak* themselves in mystery, their love of soccer, but only if they be the *ghoul-scorer,* their strange addiction to fairy tales (and *fairies' tails)*, especially *Ghould-dilocks,* their fascination with James Bond, their favorite being *Ghouled-finger* (note from Editor – enough 'ghoul' jokes).

You will discover about the education of Vampires, how they start at school by learning their *alpha-bat,* and the tragic story of the failed vampire who fainted at the *sight of blood.* You will discover about the way they fill their days, playing *badminton* and their particularly steady hands, which makes them expert *en-grave-rs.*

But this chapter is not just about Vampires, you will discover the world of Cannibals, the number who drowned when *they were fired from 17th Century War Ships;* of the successful TV show, featuring six lovable trolls living in a New York apartment block – *Fiends* - and you will learn how all these creatures from the dark have the most disgusting eating habits, *goblin* their food with no manners.

This is the most frightening chapter in the book. I understand if you wish to *vault* over it and go on to Chapter Two. But for those brave enough to remain, read on and enjoy what comes *neck-st.*

1

How many cannibals can you get in the new BMW Mini Cooper S?

Millions. They keep *eating each other!*

2

What is a vampire's favorite dessert?

Leeches and Scream!

3

What is a vampire's favorite musical?

Cats. They love the song *'Midnight'.*

4

What do you call a man with a spade in his head?

Doug.

What do you call a man without a spade in his head?

Douglas...

5

What is the perfect menu for a vampire?

Scream of Mushroom Soup

Followed by

Stake

And with a bowl of *I-Scream* for dessert.

Vein-illa of course.

He likes it all washed down with a

Bloody Mary, a *Very Bloody Mary!*

6

How did the Vampire die?

Too much *coffin!*

7

What is a vampire's favorite superhero?

***Bat*-man, of course.**

8

Where does a vampire keep his money?

In a *blood bank.*

9

Which room is the safest to be in during a zombie attack?

The *living* room!

10

How did the zombie know he was going to meet the girl of his dreams?

He read it in his *horror*scope!

11

Does a zombie eat brains with his fingers?

Yes, but he prefers the fingers...

12

What is the alcoholic drink a vampire loves the most?

Tequill-ya!

13

A fireman, a nurse and a zombie walk into a bar.

Three zombies walk out!

14

What does a vampire doctor say when he is ready to see his next patient?

Neck-st!

15

What kind of person chooses a vampire as his doctor?

A stupid one!

16

Anybody know the reason that Dracula has no friends?

Yeah, because he can be a *pain in the neck!*

17

Did you hear about the woman who decided to marry a ghost?

We don't know what *possessed her...*

18

Why do witches make the best weather forecasters?

They don't, but at least they predict a lot of *sunny spells!*

19

There was a knock on my door last Halloween. When I opened it, there was a boy dressed as a zombie and carrying a bird and clock.

***"Tick or Tweet?"* he said.**

20

A cannibal boy was chasing a missionary through the jungle. But he stopped when his mum told him to...

Stop playing with his food!

21

Why do vampires chop up their food?

They like to eat in bite sized pieces!

22

What's a vampire's favorite dance?

The *Fang*dango!

23

What's Dracula's favorite Abba song?

Fer*fang*do!

24

Did you hear about the witch who wanted to lose weight?

She joined *weight witches!*

25

Jilly the witch liked to name the items in her house. There was Chester the Chair, Barry the Bed, Nick the Knife and as the for her saucepan…

It was *called Ron!*

26

How can you spot a Cannibal in a restaurant?

He's the one who's ordered a waiter!

27

Hear about the stupid skeleton?

He was a right *bonehead!*

28

Vampires love the postman.

He delivers their *fang mail!*

29

Where is the best place to find a Zombie swimming?

In the *Dead Sea*...

30

We might criticize vampires, but they do make brilliant and loving families.

Yes, *blood is thicker than water!*

Chapter Summary

I hope that you have enjoyed this chapter. That it hasn't sent you into a *pit* of despair. Remember these key lessons:

- The referee in a match between a team of trolls and a team of cannibals is known as the ***vampire.***
- If you ever want to join the Vampire Fan club, remember to include your name, address and ***blood type*** on your application.
- And don't ever visit a vampire at 11am. They will be on their ***coffin break.***
- Never trust the author of a book on Vampires. It was probably written by a ***ghost writer.***

In the next chapter we will find some jokes about the Wild West, a time when men were men and *sheep were scared.*

Chapter Two: The Wild West

Well, howdy there folks, y'all still with me? Your *gunna* have a great time in this here chapter. There's *gunna* be loadsa *horsing* around, and y'all *gunna* (I warned you last chapter, stop saying the same joke over and over a**gun** – Ed) learns all about them darn critters in their ten-gallon hats and fast pictures. *(you know, they were so quick on the draw)*.

There ain't many cowboys left these days, unless you goes to Montana, and I ain't recommending that. Just like that darn meteorite wiped out them varmints the dinosaurs, so it was some kinda nat'ral disaster that wiped out the gun toting, swing door banging, horse riding men. But it weren't no *big rock* or even a *broke-n back mountain* what done for them. No, theys' were already on the wane, *the John Wayne* when some doggone disease sent them all to Boot Hill. *Bronco-it is*, the main symptoms, a *hoarse-ness* and a *sad-ole* mood.

But let's enjoy our memories, with a time when you shot first and asked questions only after a good ole glass of *sherry-ff.*

1

What do you call a man under a cow?

Pat!

2

Where's the shoe shop in Dodge City?

Boot Hill!

3

Why did the cowboy's mare stop neighing?

She was too *hoarse!*

4

Why did the cowboy cry?

Because his *doggone...*

5

Why should you never trust a cowboy?

They like to stirrup trouble!

6

Which English Soccer team do all cowboys support?

Spurs!

7

Why do cowboys carry big guns?

To *holster* their egos...

8

Why should we be scared of cowboys?

Because they are always trying to *cactus!*

9

Did you know that cowboys often wed their horses?

They like to *mare-ee!*

10

Cowboy Joe was captured by Injuns but, being kind folks, they promised him three wishes before scalping him. He thinks and asks for his first wish.

'I'll talk to my horse,' he says. The wish is granted, and he speaks to his horse. It trots off and comes back later with a beautiful red headed girl on its back.

The cowboy shakes his head and asks for the same wish for his second go. The horse trots off once more and comes back with a dark-haired beauty on its back. The cowboy frowns again, and says he needs to speak to his horse as his third wish.

The Injuns are confused but are men of their word and grant his wish. This time the horse returns with a blonde bombshell on its back.

Knowing the game is up, the cowboy looks at his horse and shouts:

'I said *posse!'*

11

A cowboy walks into the saloon at some God-forsaken dust bowl in the middle of nowhere. Everybody stops and looks at him. He is dressed in black from head to toe, the only color being the silver of the studs on his holster and the buckle on his belt.

He orders a whisky, drinks it, and leaves. He comes back almost immediately.

'What you no good sons of guns done with my horse?' he asked with a strong sense of rhythm. There is silence, until he hears a snigger. He pulls out his gun, throws it up, catches it, spins it around his finger and fires off six shots which make the sniggering boy dance.

'Now' says the man in black. 'I'm going to reload my gun, have another whisky, then when I goes outside my horse is gonna be there, ready to take me out of this little sh*t hole.' There is silence, and the sniggering boy creeps out. The man in black downs his drink, reloads his gun and stands up.

'Just warning you folk, if my horse ain't there, I'm gonna do what I did when this happened in Texas.' He tips his hat and leaves. The other drinkers crowd to the window, but his horse is there,

'Just tell me, man in black, what did you do when your horse was stolen in Texas?' asked one.

'Well' says the man in black 'I *walked home.'*

12

What did the cowboy say to his pencil?

***Draw*, partner.**

13

Did you hear about the cowboy who took hay to bed with him?

He thought it would feed his *night mares!*

14

The cowboy's car broke down on the highway.

It had ***Injun trouble!***

15

Cowboys make useless teachers.

The highest they can reach is *Deputy Head!*

16

Who is the poorest cowboy actor of all time?

Skint Eastwood.

17

Horses can be emotionally troubled.

So, it is important that they are kept in a *stable environment.*

18

Cowboy Pete liked to clean his teeth with gunpowder.

He also liked to *shoot his mouth off!*

19

What do you get if you mix a cowboy with a frog?

Hoppalong Cassidy!

20

Why do cowboys ride their horses?

They're too heavy *to carry*, stupid.

21

Of all the peoples who have lived in the US, cowboys are the funniest.

They are always *horsing around!*

22

Where do cowboys cook their dinner?

At *Home, On The Range!*

23

Employment Officer: So, bow legged cowboy, why did you get fired?

Bow Legged Cowboy: They said I couldn't *keep my calves together!*

24

Who is the rudest cowboy?

Wyatt *Burp!*

25

What do you get if you cross a cowboy with a goat?

Billy the Kid!

26

How do you pay if you need more cattle for your ranch?

You wait for the *Buffalo Bill...*

27

When is the worst time for a cowboy to get ill?

During the *Doc Holliday!*

28

What do Cowboys eat in the Indian Restaurant?

Kid Curry!

29

What does a cowboy get if he eats his beans too quickly?

Wild Bill *Hiccups!*

30

How do cowboys decide the result of a soccer match if the scores are level at full time?

They have a penalty *shoot out!*

Chapter Gunnery

In this chapter we have learned all about Cowboys. But, did you know that there are very few names that cowboys have?

Yep, there are just those below:

- Clint, the great Mr. Eastwood
- Squint – ***short sighted cowboys***
- Lint – ***bandaged cowboys***

- Mint – *Cowboys who clean their teeth*
- Flint – *Cowboys who live in the Rockies*
- And Hint – *do you need a clue for that one?*

Chapter Three: A Sporting Life

The joys of sport. Running about on fields, messing about in the water, getting up close in the locker room. Sport covers everything, from events where we look on in awe at the competitors, such as the *Admire all's* **Cup,** to factory floor sports, like *boxing,* to the 200 in a court carnage that is *squash.* Bunch of *vegetables* play that!

1

What's an insect's favorite sport?

Cricket!

2

Which football team fly to all their matches, even home ones?

The New York *Jets!*

3

Which are the noisiest sports players?

Tennis players. They create such a *racket*...

4

And just to prove that *ALL* our jokes are fresh and original....

Which are the other noisiest sports players?

Badminton players. They create such a *racket!*

5

Which is the maddest sport?

Table Tennis. The players are *bat*-ty.

6

Which sport makes you scratch?

Quidd – *itch.*

7

Which sportsmen and women are best at Do It Yourself?

Throwers – they are good with *hammers!*

8

Which sport is most like a breaking down car?

Shot *putt...putt...putt...putt...*

9

Did you hear the football coach shouting at the vending machine?

He was shouting '*Give me my quarter back!*'

10

I arranged a date at the gym with my girlfriend, but she didn't show up.

We didn't *work out*...

11

Why do so many pregnant women go to the gym?

They're *body building!*'

12

Remember, even the best commentators are only...

Average potatoes!

13

Why are referees so much in demand for soccer matches in Africa?

To deal with all the *cheetahs!*

14

Which dog is best in a fight?

A boxer!

15

Which Simon and Garfunkel song is most likely to be a hit?

"The Boxer"!

16

I've just eaten a bowl of cornflakes.

Does that make me a *cereal killer?*

17

I just discovered that my wife is color blind.

The news came right out the *yellow!*

18

Drowning is certainly dangerous…

But is still *breath taking!*

19

A banana went to the doctors.

It wasn't *peeling* well.

20

Why is it better to be addicted to brake fluid than an alcoholic?

At least with the brake fluid, you can *stop* when you want to.

21

Which fairy tale character is the most useless at soccer?

Cinderella, she always runs away *from the ball!*

22

Swimming trunks…

The result of a love affair between a fish and an elephant.

23

Why did the snooker player get wet?

He kept looking for the *pool!*

24

Why did the athlete get into trouble?

I don't know, but he was certainly for the *high jump!*

25

Baseball...

An alternative *testicle!*

26

Why did the batsman warm up his neck so carefully?

He didn't want to *cricket!*

27

Why should you never swim on a full stomach?

Because you should always swim in *water!*

28

Horse racing…

Running with a *sore throat.*

29

Is History a sport?

No, it's a *past-time!*

30

How do pool players pay for their groceries?

They join the *cue*...

Chapter Swimmery

In this chapter we have certainly learned that sport is no *laughing matter.* Remember the following points, and sport will be a useful and worthwhile part of your life.

- Train properly for sport, the **7.32 from New York to Philadelphia** is particularly good for this.
- Treat your opponents with sportsmanship and respect, unless they **beat you.**
- Do not commit fouls or break the rules; if you find this hard try to find fixtures against teams of nuns. That will help you to *kick the habit.*

In the next chapter you will learn the joys of Christmas, Thanksgiving and other festivals. Although I personally get fed up with all the prickly green foliage we need to hang up every *holly day.*

Chapter Four: Celebrations and Other Festivals

In this chapter you will learn about all kinds of festivals. Why you should never take your turkey to Church at Christmas – they use *fowl* **language.** How you need to save up for Thanksgiving soup – well it is made of 16 *carrots.* And why, tragically, the last words of every turkey are, *'I'm stuffed.'*

1

What's the best place to go on holiday at Thanksgiving?

Turkey!

2

If April showers bring May flowers, what do May flowers bring?

Pilgrims!

3

What did the turkey say to the cook as the feast was being prepared?

Quack!

4

Turkeys are not very clever. We found ours sitting on a tomahawk…

He was trying to hatchet!

5

How is Thanksgiving always finished?

With the letter *G!*

6

Which animal makes the best percussionist?

None are that good, but a least a Turkey has its own *drumsticks!*

7

Why did the turkey cross the road?

The chicken needs a break sometimes.

8

Contrary to popular belief, America was actually discovered by a cat.

Christopher-y Columbus!

9

Google. Google. Google.

A turkey on a computer.

10

After coming over from wet and cold England, did the Pilgrims get sun burned when they landed in America?

No, just a *Puritan!*

11

Pilgrimage…

The age of a *Pilgrim.*

12

Fangs-giving…

A vampire's favorite day *of the year!*

13

What kind of turkey needs an exorcism?

A *poultry-gheist!*

14

How do you serve wine to a turkey?

In a *goblet!*

15

Why are dad's jokes so good at Christmas?

Because he tells real *crackers!*

16

What's the best place to go on holiday at Christmas?

Brussels!

17

What do film directors say when making movies about Christmas presents?

OK. We're done. It's a *wrap.*

18

Which illness does Santa Claus suffer from?

Tinsil-it is!

19

What do you call people who are scared of Santa?

Claus-trophobic!

20

English grammar – what is a subordinate clause?

One of *Santa's little helpers.*

21

What happens if you sit in the snow for too long.

You develop *polaroids!*

22

How do you know if there's a snowman in your bed?

You wake up wet!

23

What's the difference between a snowboard student and a snowboard instructor?

About six hours!

24

What do you call a stupid Easter bunny?

Hare-brained!

25

What else do you call a stupid Easter bunny?

Anything you like, it's a *bunny!*

26

Why are bunnies like calculators?

They both *multiply quickly!*

27

Never fall in love with a pastry chef, even on Valentine's Day...

He'll *dessert* you!

28

Chat up line for a math teacher:

If you were an angle, you'd be *acute* one!

29

What's the difference between a $10 bunch of flowers, and a $60 bunch of flowers?

February 14th !

Two teens chatting in the cafeteria. Jock: Hey, do you have a date for Valentine's day?

Geek: Yes, *February 14th*!

Chapter Wintry

So, what has this chapter taught us?

- If giving a gift, do it now, in the ***present.***
- Always give your Easter gift on time, you don't want it to be **choco*late.***
- And remember, if there is a war, make sure your Christmas tree signs up quickly. After all, it's covered in ***decorations.***

Next, we will learn how food lovers make the best doctors, they provide people with an ***epic cure.***

Chapter Five: The Best Medicine, Food And Drink

This chapter was hard to write – it touched my *art. I choke* even now as I consider the *grape* burden I carry. You see, my mother never breast fed me, she told me she only wanted me as a *friend.* Enough, I *carrot* go on with this anymore. Like dinner at my brother's, it's time for *gags.*

1

What do film directors eat on a shoot?

They love a *wrap!*

2

What's orange and sounds like a parrot?

A *Carrot.*

3

What's a photographer's favorite food?

Cheese...

4

Why was the fungi squashed on the plate?

Because it didn't have *mushroom*...

5

Never have a discussion with a waffle.

It can't get to the point.

6

Pie-jamas…

Clothes for a *midnight feast!*

7

Pilau…

Something to sleep on after *a curry*.

8

A baked potato walks into a bar.

'Get out' says the barman 'we don't *serve food here!*'

9

Obesity?

It's just a *snaccident.*

10

Coffee – one of life's victims…

It's always being *mugged.*

11

When we finally develop the ability to colonize Mars, we won't build any restaurants.

They'll lack *atmosphere!*

12

A swarm of termites go into a saloon.

They ask: 'Is the *bar tender* here?'

13

There's no food in the Italian restaurant today.

The cook *pastaway*...

14

Lemonade...

When a Lemon helps out.

Orangeade...

When an orange helps out.

Limeade…

When a lime helps out.

Gatorade…

Don't trust it!

15

My mother in law is a terrible cook.

Her signature dish is *indigestion*.

16

When dad tells a joke in the cinema.

It's *pop corn*.

When I was young, I had to eat worms every day to survive.

I still thank my *brother for saving my life!*

The bully who used to steal my lunch money at school still takes it today.

But he makes a great *Subway!*

Bacon causes cancer. Smoking causes cancer.

But smoking bacon *cures it.*

20

Life's a bitch. One day you're the best thing since sliced bread.

The next, *you're toast!*

21

What's the difference between a forty-year-old single dad and an egg?

Eggs get *laid!*

22

We just held a pistachio themed fancy dress party.

It was *nuts!*

23

I saw my dad chopping onions today and I cried.

He was my *favorite hamster!*

24

Sea gull = a bird flying over the sea…

Bagel = a bird flying over the *bay*…

25

My girlfriend's just lied to me. She told me that she didn't have a date.

And I've just seen her *eating one!*

26

Our clock was hungry.

It went back *four seconds!*

27

Question: Define the word imposter.

Answer: *False Pasta.*

28

I have a friend whose vegetarian. And a transgender. He's called Chuck now but used to be Rosemary.

He's a man now, but he was an *herb-before!*

29

The student ate his easy homework.

It was a *piece of cake!*

30

My neighbor's star sign was cancer. That was pretty ironic given how he died.

Imagine, being *eaten by a giant crab!*

Chapter Fruitery

You have learned a lot about food in this chapter. But here is the biggest lesson of all.

- If your wife packs you a salad for lunch...**it's time to get her some flowers.**
- If somebody else buys her flowers...**it's time to start eating salads for lunch.**

In the next chapter we will consider music, film and other cultural matters. We will come across some great writers and singers, such and that duo made up of a close relation, **Simon and**

Garth's Uncle; the playwrite who made threatening gestures with a deadly weapon, **William *Shakespeare*** and Dan Brown.

Chapter Six: If Music Be The Food Of Love, Then Joke On

And now for our cultural, classical section. We will examine Maurice's drawings. Yes, *Mozart* will feature. We will look at one of the most popular writers in the world's new venture into horror stories, yes, *John Gruesome's* books really are gruesome. We will even consider the work of the most prejudiced songwriter of all time. Yes, not even *Joan Bias* will escape our scrutiny.

1

What is a film director's favorite type of music?

Rap!

(Note: Three jokes with the same theme – this one, the Christmas present one and the food one; that's premier league dad-joke classic behavior. Tell them one after the other to really annoy your family.)

2

Which singers are most useful at Christmas?

Rappers...

3

My printer is really advanced, it even plays music.

Yes, the *paper keeps jamming.*

4

Peter Pan, a story about a boy who flies everywhere

In fact, he *Neverlands.*

5

Software writers never write their game programs in the garden.

There are too many *bugs!*

6

The set designer on the new Broadway hit got the sack.

Still, he *didn't make a scene.*

7

When the actor forgot his lines:

It was *curtains* for him!

8

Guardians of the Galaxy...

Starring the *security staff in Samsung* shops.

9

Why did the Jedi cross the road at night?

To get to the *Dark Side!*

10

Why did the Star Wars' cast duck?

Because they saw *Hans Solo!*

11

My friend has just joined a blonds only theatre group.

Still, *fair play* to him.

12

I know somebody who is really into Amateur Dramatics, but he keeps jumping through the floor.

We hope it's just a *stage he's going through.*

13

How do stars arrive at the Academy Awards?

By Os*car!*

14

What's Beethoven's favorite fruit?

Ba-na-na-naaa...

15

There are so many good jokes about composers.

You could compile a *Liszt!*

16

Musician: Disaster, darling, I've broken my brass instrument!

Conductor: That's OK, I'll lend you a *tuba glue!*

17

What happens if you drop a piano down a mine shaft?

You get *A flat Minor.*

18

Why couldn't the opera singer get into her house?

She couldn't find the right *key.*

19

What's the definition of perfect pitch?

When you throw a rock and *it hits your six-year old's violin!*

20

How did writers drink their tea in medieval times?

Out of a cup and *Chaucer*.

21

Why did the actor break his leg?

It was the only way he could get into a *cast*.

22

A young actor won his first part in a play. He was cast as a husband.

His family were very encouraging, and his father said:

'If you keep working hard, one day you'll get a *speaking part*.'

23

Who was the greatest actor from biblical times?

Samson, *he brought the house down!*

24

Appearing on the stage is the easiest job in the world.

It's all *play.*

25

I went to a book store and asked the sales person where to find the 'Self-help' section.

She *told me to find it.*

26

Why did Adele cross the road?

To sing '*Hello from the Other Side*'!

27

Harry Potter…

Clay work for the Hirsute!

28

How do you get out of Hogwarts?

Through the Dumble-*door!*

29

A dell…

The singing *computer.*

30

An observation of Donald Trump's administration: We used to have Johnny Cash, Steve Jobs and Bob Hope.

Now, we've *no cash, no jobs and no hope!*

Chapter Drummery

This chapter has helped to turn you into a cultural icon. Or at least, **I conned** you into thinking that. To make your education complete, here are some books you must read.

- Lewis Carroll by ***Alison Wonderland***
- Did O.J. Do It? By ***Howard I Know***
- The Growth of the French Population by ***Francis Crowded***
- I lived in New York by ***Helen Earth***
- The Most Deadly Animal Illnesses by ***Ann Thrax***
- Leo Tolstoy by ***Warren Peace***

- Embarrassing Clothing by *Leah Tard.*

Next, we will cast our mind over that most misogynistic of school subjects, *History.*

Chapter Seven: History – The Tragic Tale Of Mankind

Yes, history. Humanity's most difficult moment. A time full of tyrants, where nobody remembered the ordinary man. A time of war and political corruption. **Thank goodness that's all in the past.**

1

Which US monument is always in a hurry?

Mount *Rushmore!*

2

Which civilization travelled the most?

The *Roam*-ans.

3

Which US President was…

The best timekeeper? *Eyes on Hour.*

The cleanest? *Washington.*

The best gardener? *Bush* **(either of them although George W sometimes gets lost in the vegetable patch).**

The best alien warrior? *Ray-gun.*

Most full of wind? *Trump.*

The best cleaner? *Hoover.*

The grooviest, man? **Why, *Cool*-idge of course.**

The best jam maker? *Fillmore.*

The best handyman? *Tyler.*

The worst? **Richard Nixon, no pun intended.**

4

Moses makes the best tea out of anybody from history.

Hebrews **it!**

5

Feminism over the ages.

Herstory…

6

The dark ages.

A time when the world was full of *knights!*

7

One of the greatest times in American History – the Stamp Act.

Yeah, we certainly *licked the British!*

8

Camelot…

A place to *park your camel!*

9

What are history teachers' favorite food?

Dates!

10

And what do history teachers talk about when they are in the bar?

The *good old days.*

11

Did you know that the planet's biggest heist was carried out by Atlas?

He *held up the entire world!*

12

Liberty...

Tea for the *American Colonists!*

13

When King Arthur wanted a round table he visited the best carpenter in ancient Britain.

Sir Cumference!

14

Norse Code…

The way *the Vikings communicated at sea!*

15

Ancient Greece…

Flavors your French Fries!

16

Did you hear about the invention of the wheel?

It caused a *revolution!*

17

Where did they sign the Declaration of Independence?

At the *bottom!*

18

What did German pilots eat for breakfast during the Second World War?

Luftwaffles!

19

Do you know why Renoir became an Impressionist?

He did it for the *Monet!*

20

And, was Renoir a good Impressionist?

So-so, but he did an excellent *Donald Trump!*

B

What's a snake's favorite school subject?

Hissstory.

22

Lafayette…

The biggest *joker in Washington's army!*

23

If only we'd listen the first time…

History wouldn't need to *keep repeating itself!*

24

Do you know why the Pilgrims sailed to America in the Spring?

Because *April Showers bring May Flowers!*

25

Why couldn't the whale digest Jonah?

Because you can't *keep a good man down!*

26

Floodlights…

Invented by *Noah for the Ark.*

27

Most skilled worker in the bible?

Noah – he was a brilliant *arkitecht!*

28

Which king invented fractions?

Henry the Seventh!

29

What is two um plus two um?

A *forum!*

30

What did the student say when he failed History?

'Best let *bygones be bygones.'*

Chapter Done Already

So, there is the history of the world, told in thirty gags. Time to cheers and celebrate. Which reminds me of the time a Roman Centurion went into a bar.

'A martinus, please' he ordered.

'Don't you mean *martini*?' inquired the barman.

'If I'd have wanted a *double* I'd have ordered one,' replied the soldier.

The next chapter is very important, very serious. In it we consider some of the serious matters of life – health, education, legal rights, Grey's Anatomy – I can't believe that they're writing Arizona out of the show, I mean, where will it go next? It's still recovering from losing Derek and Christina…

Chapter Eight: Medicine, Education And Law – A Professional Chapter

In this chapter you will learn about the importance of when you become a judge, not being *court,* and that if you are bad, you might well get sent to school, **to *learn your lesson.***

1

Doctor, doctor, I feel like a pair of curtains.

Sit down and *pull yourself together.*

2

Doctor, Doctor, I feel like a new man.

Hmm, here's my password for *Grindr.*

3

Here's a new job. Cyclologist.

A shrink who *enjoys exercise!*

4

Doctor, Doctor, I feel like I'm dead.

Hmm, are you doing a lot of *coffin?*

5

'Hey teacher!'

'Yes Johnnie?'

'You wouldn't shout at me for something I haven't done, would
you?'

'No Johnnie.'

Well, *I haven't done my homework…*

6

Sir, I can't come to your lesson today, I'm ill, I feel like a pack of cards.

Go outside, I'll *deal with you* later!

7

A small child was rushed to hospital after she swallowed ten toy horses from her toy farm.

Fortunately, her condition is now *stable!*

8

Doctor, Doctor, I'm really ill, I've got a strawberry growing out of my head.

Umm, you'll need some *cream for that!*

9

An elementary school class are talking about their ambitions in life. One boy wants to be a banker, another to be a soldier. One of the girls has the goal to become a surgeon and another to be a teacher.

When it comes to little Johnny's turn he says: 'I want to win ten million dollars on the lottery just like my parents did.'

The teacher is open mouthed. 'Your parents won ten million dollars on the lottery!' she repeats.

'No' says Johnny, 'but they *wanted to!'*

10

Don't become a vegetarian...

It's a big *missed steak!*

11

Why did the student want to find out why the world rotates?

He knew it would *make his day*.

12

The math book is looking really sad.

It has so many *problems!*

13

After being hit by a car, a man was rushed to hospital. The doctors looked in horror at his injuries.

'There's only one thing we can do' said the surgeon to his worried wife.

'What's that?' asked the wife nervously.

'Well, you can see how he was hit by the car,' continued the surgeon. 'We'll have to operate and amputate his left ear, left arm and left leg.'

'Will he be *all right* then?' asked the wife.

14

A woman goes to the Doctor for her annual check-up. The Doctor takes her blood pressure, her pulse, her heart rate and her temperature. He looks concerned.

'I have to say that the problem is that you are obese' he tells the patient.

The woman is shocked. 'I want a second opinion' she says.

'OK' says the doctor *'you're ugly too.'*

15

What do you call a blind fish?

A *fsh*.

16

Skeletons. They are terrible liars.

You can *see right through them!*

17

How do you spot a blind man on a beach?

It's *never that hard* really!

18

Retail therapy…

Shopping for dogs who've *lost their tails.*

19

Our dog likes sitting on sandpaper.

It makes him go '*Ruff*'!

20

Why don't skeletons ever get dates?

They don't have *the guts* to ask!

21

A major crime spree has been ended with the arrest of two commas, a full stop, thirty consonants and ten vowels.

They will be sentenced next week.

22

A man goes to the Doctor to get the results of his medical tests. The Doctor looks serious and tells the man to sit down.

'I'm very sorry to tell you' he says 'that the news isn't good. You've only got ten to live.'

The man is shocked. He thought he only had an ingrowing toe nail. Then he realizes what the Doctor has said.

'Ten? Ten what? Ten years, ten months? Is it just ten weeks?

The Doctor looks at him, and says, slowly.

'Nine...'

23

How do you tell the difference between a snowman and a snow woman?

Check for *snowballs!*

Little Jimmy came home from school looking very happy.

'Did you have a good day, darling?' asked his mum.

'We certainly did' said Jimmy. 'We made explosives in science.'

'Gosh' his mother replied 'you do have exciting lessons these days. And what will you be doing at school tomorrow?'

Jimmy gives a knowing smile. *'School? What school?'*

Chapter Summarily

Bullying is no laughing matter, so here is a little story that won't make you laugh.

In the morning Johnny calls to his mother.
'Mummy,' he says, 'I don't feel well. Do I have to go to school today?'
His mother asks him what is wrong.
'I don't like school,' he says. 'The children bully me; the teachers hate me, and I never get my work right. Please can I stay at home?'
Mother looks him in the eye.

'No Johnny, you're the *Principal*'

In the next chapter you will learn a lot less than you did in this one, if that is possible. After all, this chapter had a section about teachers. Next is a chapter on single cruise ships, sometimes known as *one liners.*

Chapter Nine: Apple – A Fruit You Have To Tug

In this chapter we will look at one liners. Jokes made up of one, **two or three sentences.**

1

My new daughter was born the other day. It was a bit sad, she had a large round head and was a bit yellow. Yes, *Melanie* is a bit strange looking.

2

My local churchman has a lot of strange pets. He's got a lion, a tiger, a leopard and a jaguar. Yes, he's a *cat-a-holic.*

3

Two nuns are in a bath. Don't ask why. One asks the other 'Where's the soap?'

'Yes, *it does'* the other agrees.

4

The gas fire fell out with the radiator. **They had a *heated* argument.**

5

Tulips.

The best flower *to kiss!*

6

Beard.

Facial hair for *lager.*

7

Did you hear about the surgeon who tricked his patient?

It was a right *stitch up!*

8

I-gloo.

The way the Inuit people *stick their homes together.*

9

Cement.

The way sex addicts *stick their homes together!*

10

Mortar.

The way soldiers *stick their homes together.*

11

Tongue and Groove

The way sexy dancers *stick their homes together.*

(enough of these, please! Ed.)

12

Nails.

The way beauticians *stick their homes together.*

(I've told you – no more 'sticking a home together joke⸀

13

Did you read in the science journal? A disaster! The noble gasses…

Argon!

(That's better, I don't get it but at least it's not about construction.)

14

The dog thought he saw a squirrel in the branches.

But he was *barking up the wrong tree.*

15

Three arguing teenagers sitting in a boat.

Two *fell out!*

16

Films we'd like to see…

Indiana Jones and the Strange Animal.

Or

Raiders of the Lost *Aardvark*.

Begin dismantling the space ship.

Or

Start Wreck.

Undercover White House.

Or

Casa Blan*ket*.

Fruit takes over the world.

Or

Planet of the *Grapes*.

Horror on two wheels.

Or

Psych*le*.

A History of Surgery.

Or

Back to the *Suture*.

Killer Chocolate Bars.

Or

Mars Attacks.

A Very Serious Film Indeed.

Or

Gravity.

Rudeness in Space.

Or

De*pravity.*

17

I still miss my ex-girlfriend, but **I'm working on my** *aim.*

18

My socks are so holey I can *wear them to church!*

19

Hear about the attractive woman who undresses in the bathroom? She's so beautiful she *turns the shower on...*

20

Hey, try searching on the web for 'ways to start a fire'. You get **millions of *matches!***

21

Ireland has the fastest growing capital city in the world.

Every year it's *Dublin.*

22

Never go out with a cross eyed person.

They're seeing someone *on the side.*

23

Do you know the worst job in the world?

Working for a calendar company. *You never get a day off.*

24

Bored to death?

You've just been *killed by a pig.*

25

Never a tell a joke about the unemployed.

They *don't work.*

26

I picked up a one-legged hitchhiker the other day.

I told him to *hop in.*

27

Winnie the Pooh?

The result of breeding a bear with a skunk.

28

Boo-bees...

When you need *milk, not honey.*

29

Jokes about menstruation are not funny.

Period!

30

My dogs got no nose.

How does he smell?

Terrible!

31

Join the fire service, a *warm welcome guaranteed.*

32

Velcro…

Nothing but a big *rip off!*

33

Why did the Sea Anemone blush?

He'd just seen the ocean's *bottom.*

34

Why is the top of a set of traffic lights always red?

It gets embarrassed when it sees the *green light changing.*

35

Why did the tomato blush?

It saw the salad *dressing.*

36

'Mummy, mummy, I want a space party for my birthday!'

'Ok, but you'll have to *planet.* '

37

They're selling TV's for five dollars each in a shop down the road. They're perfect, except the volume controls are stuck.

Get there quick, it's an offer you *can't turn down!*

38

Atoms. The world's biggest liars.

They make up *everything!*

39

Arms – man's best friend.

They're always by *your side!*

40

A man sued an airline company after they misplaced his luggage.

But he *lost his case.*

41

We're going to Mississippi this summer.

We haven't seen Mr. Hippy and *his wife* for months!

42

What's a law suit?

An *attorney's smart clothes*.

43

I'm delighted.

Somebody *stole my torch!*

44

My wife? It's tricky to say what she does.

She sells sea shells on the sea shore.

45

I telephoned the spiritual leader of Tibet the other day. He sent me a large goat with a long neck.

Turns out I'd phoned *'Dial a Llama.'*

46

I'd like to retrain as an Australian psychiatrist, because it is such an easy job.

G'day, G'day, how you doing? No worries, next.

47

Militant feminists, I take my hat off to them.

They *don't like that.*

48

They've just turned the old kebab shop into a Chinese Restaurant, because the old owner died.

Now he's *turning in his grave!*

49

I was playing chess in the street when the police arrested me.

I said, *'It's because I'm black, isn't it?'*

My grandfather invented the cold air balloon.

It *never really took off*.

Chapter Funnery

There you go with 50 one-liners, or one fifty liner, if you prefer.

A few warnings, though if you are thinking of publishing your own joke book.

- If it's for a Scotsman, it will need to be checked carefully; **they like to *print on tartan*.**
- Don't follow my mistake when I wrote a book on horses. **Paper *works much better*.**
- The guy who wrote Mary Poppins had a problem as well. He had to work so closely on the text that he developed *Umdiddlediddlediddleumdiddly Eye*.

Next, we will prove that long jokes can be just as unfunny as short ones.

Chapter Ten: Long Jokes

The long joke, the War and Peace of comedy. They're great, as long as they don't start *once a pun a time*.

1

The Wasp Joke. The world's greatest gag?

A man goes into a baker's. He looks at the lovely array of breads and cakes on offer and waits his turn.

'Yes, sir? What can I get you?' asks the shop assistant when it is his turn.

'I would like a loaf of soda bread, a strawberry tart and a wasp, please.'

'Well, I can get you the soda bread, and the strawberry tarts are an excellent choice,' replies the shop assistant with a confused look on his face. 'But the wasp?'

'Yes,' states the customer.

'I've just seen one in your *window!*'

2

The Politically Incorrect Joke

Three men are sitting on a park bench. Life has looked badly on them. Jim is homeless, his lovely four bed condo lost after a life of gambling. Jed is a druggie. He'd love to stop, but the attraction is too great. Joe is an alcoholic. He is quite happy with his lot. And even happier with his bottle of Jack Daniels.

Jed and Jim are discussing how bad their existence is – Joe is in a drunken stupor – when there is a rushing noise from a nearby tree. A fairy wearing a sparkly green dress and carrying a glowing magic wand suddenly appears.

'Life has not treated you well,' she says to the startled threesome. 'But I believe that you want to make amends. I will grant each of you three wishes, but, this will be your last chance. Use them wisely.

The three men are astonished. Could this be true?

'Jim. You first,' offers the kindly but mysterious sprite.

'OK,' he says. 'I guess I'd like my family back.'

In a flash the word 'Daddy' is heard and looking up he sees a small girl skipping across the park towards him. Behind, smiling is a beautiful woman pushing a pram.

'Wow,' he breathes. 'Then, next, I'd like a lovely house.'

This time there is a crash. In the corner of the park, a beautiful home suddenly appears, with a white painted fence, swings in the garden and smoke lazily appearing from the chimney.

None of the three can believe it. Joe is so shocked he downs the rest of his Jack Daniels in one, long glug.

'Look,' says Jim, 'I've blown it once, and I don't want to a second time. Please make me never gamble again.' A bright light shines over his head, and suddenly Jim knows that life will be better. He waves to his companion, thanks the fairy and, holding the hand of his smiling daughter, joins his wife as they head to their perfect home.

'Now for you,' says the fairy to Jed. 'Simply remember, use your wishes wisely.'

'I think if I had a job, I'd be less likely to go back on drugs.'

A flash of light brightens him, and his old, smelly coat is gone. Now he is wearing a smart business suit, a brief case at his knee and from his pocket comes the sound of an email dropping into his top of the range iPhone.

'You know, I've always wanted a great car.'

'Simple.' The fairy waves her hand and the sound of a door closing is heard behind him.

'Here are your keys,' comes the voice of the car salesman. Jed looks up and there, behind the smiling man, is a bright, red, gleaming Jaguar.

'This is unreal. But, like Jim, I don't want to ever end up back where I am today,' gasps Jed. 'Please fairy, make the thought of drugs a horror to me.'

And instantly, he knows he will never take them again. He collects his keys and heads off to his new office.

'And finally, Joe, your three wishes. Remember, use them wisely.'

Joe looks at wistfully at the empty bottle of Jack Daniels in his hand.

'Just imagine, if I always had a drink ready. I would like a never-ending bottle of Jack Daniels,' he says.

Suddenly, he feels the weight of the full bottle. He takes a gulp and looks down. As he watches, the bottle refills. He drinks once more, downing a quarter of the drink. A big smile appears on his face as the bottle fills again.

'You know,' he says, 'I think I'll have *two more of these!*'

3

An inflatable boy got a place in the country's best inflatable school. His inflatable teachers worked hard and thought that the boy was happy. But he wasn't. One day he took a pin to school, and punctured the school, his teachers and finally, in an act of guilty sacrifice, stabbed himself.

His Principal was furious and called the deflated boy into his deflated office.

'I can't believe your behavior,' he roared. *'You've let your teachers down, your school down and most of all, yourself, down.'*

4

A duck goes into a bar. He waddles up to the barman and orders a beer. The barman pours his beer in astonishment, takes the duck's cash and hands over the change without a word. The duck looks hard at the change, puts it away, and downs his drink.

When he is finished, he sees that the barman is still staring at him.

'You don't get many ducks in here, do you?' he says.

Still amazed, the barman replies: 'No, we don't.'

The duck looks at his empty glass.

'I'm not surprised at those prices,' he says.

5

A pretentious couple head into a bar.

'A glass of your finest H20' says the woman, with an arrogant chuckle.

The bartender pulls a bottle out of the fridge, pours it out and looks with a resigned expression at the woman's partner.

'Oh, he'll have H20 too,' she said.

She is now serving life without parole. The barman's serving with a smile.

It's all in the name...

Dan – the man with a black belt in judo.

June – Sandy girl.

Bill – the man who's expensive to take out to lunch.

Sidney – the man from Australia.

Michael – the man who buys his round.

Noelle – Or, Noee as she likes to be known.

Aiden – the man who always helps.

Logan – the man who starts computers.

Ruth – keeps the rain out.

Nina – the ambulance.

Carmen – the mechanic.

John – the man in the toilet.

Luke – the other man in the toilet.

Dillan – herbman.

Andrew – the artist.

Levi – the man with the jeans.

Nora – loves a good chew.

Owen – the man in debt.

Grayson – the boring child.

Isaiah – he looks down on you.

Rebecca – Becca again.

Thomas – the cat's anus.

Connor – don't trust him.

Parker – get him to put your car away.

Adam – good in a flood.

Sawyer – great at hide and seek.

Ryder – good on a horse.

Elias – never tells the truth.

Carlos – he's happy to walk.

Weston – the star of cowboy films.

Abel – he's good!

7

The French Farmer Joke

A French farmer has a problem with rats. It doesn't matter how many traps he sets, how much poison he puts down, they still keep eating his sacks of meal and generally causing issues.

In despair, he asks his wife if she has any ideas. That shows how desperate he is. *(Only say that line out loud if you are very brave or in male only company!)*

His wife replies *(in a French accent):* 'Yes, I sink you shord geet some cats, les chats'

'Breelient,' he replies 'Zat's zee beest idea you eff ed since you agreed to marry moi'

So, he heads to the cat shop and buys three cats. He takes them home and tells his wife.

'I eff brought tree cats'

'Tree cats, like leopards?'

'Non, non, tree cats, you know, one two tree. But I do not know vwot to call zem.'

'Ah, I eff an idea' says the wife 'You should call zem Un, Deux and Trois'

'Ok' replies the farmer 'zat is not so good as you last idea, but it is still good enough. Ah shall call zem "Un, Deux and Trois" '

125

But the cats are rubbish at rat hunting. They just sit all day in the sun, and if a rat comes along they just purr even more loudly. The farmer is so cross with them that, in a fit of rage he grabs the cats, puts them in a bag, ties the top and throws them into the well. Then he feels guilty and decides to keep his act secret. But after a few days his wife begins to wonder where they are.

'Darling' she asks the farmer eventually 'vere are zee cats? I ef not zeen zem for zeveral days'

The farmer looks serious and decides that he must tell the truth.

'I ef a confession' he says 'ze cats are dead. Yes, *Un Deux Trois Quatre Cinq...'*

8

A Poem

I dig

You dig

We dig

They dig

Some dig

All dig

Go dig

Say dig

OK, it might not sound great, but

It's very *deep!*

9

A hotel owner is in despair. All his guests are thieves. Whenever he gets the maid to load up the free soap, free gel, free shampoo and so on in the rooms they are always gone by the next day.

He tries everything, leaving notes, putting out bigger containers that could not possibly be used up, but whatever he does, the soap, shampoo and shower gels are always gone.

He can only reach one conclusion.

His guests are a bunch of *dirty bastards!*

10

A woman is in the bath when her doorbell rings. She calls out to ask who it is.

'I'm just the blind man' comes the reply.

So, the woman decides she can safely answer the door. She gets out the bath and drips her way across the carpet to the front door.

She opens the door. The man whistles.

'Nice tits, now where do you *want the blind?*

Chapter Symmetry – a balanced report...

Look, some stories are too serious to be funny. So, serious faces everybody. Before I was a joke writer I worked for some years with the United Nations. It was a terrible job, because I was a forensic biologist, so I was sent into some of the most appalling war zones to find out what had been going on. My worst day was when I was shown the mass grave of ten thousand snowmen. Fortunately, it turned out to be *a field of carrots.*

Our next chapter is full of knock-knock jokes. Which reminds me that I was watching that movie where a postman and a married woman plan to kill off the husband. You know, the Postman Always Rings Twice. It resonates with me because my own wife ran off with a mechanic. He too was a *male worker.* Anyway, I was sitting at home yesterday when I heard:

Knock Knock

Who's there?

It's the Postman...

Chapter Eleven: Who's That Knocking On My Door?

My doorbell plays 'Lose Yourself' by Eminem. Yeah, once he *rapped on my door...*

1

Knock Knock

'Who's there?'

'Theresa.'

'Theresa who?'

'Theresa *Green*.'

2

Knock Knock

'Who's there?'

'Theresa.'

'Theresa who?'

'Theresa Brown. It's *winter*.'

3

Knock Knock

'Who's there?'

'Banana.'

'Banana who?'

Knock Knock

'Who's there?'

'Banana'

'Banana who?'

Knock Knock

'Who's there?'

'Banana'

'Banana who?'

Knock Knock

'Who's there?'

'Orange.'

'Orange who?'

'*Orange* you glad it's not another banana?'

4

Knock Knock

'Who's there?'

'Twitter'

'Twitter who?

'Is there an *owl* around here?

5

Knock Knock

'Who's there?'

'Boo!'

'Boo who?'

'No need to *cry*!'

6

Knock Knock

'Who's there?'

'H'

'H who?'

'Bless you.'

7

Knock Knock

'Who's there?'

'The interrupting cow'

'The interrupting co...'

'Moo'

8

Knock Knock

'Who's there?'

'Opportunity'

'Don't lie to me. Opportunity *never knocks twice.*'

9

Knock Knock

'Who's there?'

'Double'

'Double who?

'No, it's *W*'

10

Knock Knock

'Who's there?'

'It's the Yoda lady'

'The Yoda lady who?'

'Wow, can you teach ME how to *yodel?*'

11

(in a threatening, dark voice)

Why did the Chicken cross the road?

'I don't know, why *did* the chicken cross the road?'

'To hunt somebody down!'

Knock Knock

'Who's there?'

'It's the chicken…'

12

Knock Knock

'Who's there?'

'Deja'

'Deja who?'

'Knock Knock'

13

Knock Knock

'Who's there?'

'Leaf'

'Leaf who?'

'I've just bought this house. Time to *leaf*'

14

Knock Knock

'Who's there?'

'Beats'

'Beats who?'

'Beats me?'

15

Knock Knock

'Who's there?'

'The extra terrestial'

135

'The extra-terrestrial who?'

'Who do you think? *How many extra terrestials do you know?'*

OR…

16

Knock Knock

'Who's there?'

'The considerate lawyer'

'The considerate lawyer who?'

'How many considerate lawyers do you know?'

OR EVEN…

17

Knock Knock

'Who's there?'

'The honest politician'

The honest politician who?

'How many honest politicians do you know?'

18

Knock Knock

'Who's there?'

'FBI'

'FB…?'

'Shut up. We're *asking the questions here.'*

19

Knock Knock

'Who's there?'

'Tiss'

'Tiss who?

'It's ok, I've already got one.'

20

Knock Knock

'Who's there?'

'Urine'

'Urine who?'

'Piss open the door, or *urine trouble*'

21

Knock Knock

'Who's there?'

'Kenya'

'Kenya who?'

'Kenya feel the lo-oove tonight?'

22

Knock Knock

'Who's there?'

'The interrupting sloth'

'The interrupting sloth who?'

'Yes'

'Who are you?'

Long pause

'Please tell me who you are'

Another pause

'I'm shutting the door in ten seconds'

'Ten'

'Nine'

'Eight'

'Seven'

'Six'

'Five'

'Four'

'Three'

'Two'

'One'

He begins to shut the door

'Sloth.'

23

Knock Knock

'Who's there?'

'Grandpa?'

'Grandpa wh....*woah, quick, someone open the coffin*'

24

Knock Knock

'Who's there?'

'I've just been to Malib'

'I've just been to Malib who?

'Nice, isn't it?'

25

Knock Knock

'Who's there?'

'Spell'

'Spell who?

'W-H-O'

26

'Look, I've got to go away.'

'Oh no, why?'

'It's my job, they're posting me overseas.'

'That's so sad. How long will you be gone?'

'Five years!'

'No! But I love you.'

'And I love you. The important thing is, you'll always remember me, won't you?'

'Of course. Always'

'That's good. Knock knock'

'Who's there?'

'Well, thanks a million'

27

Knock Knock

'Who's there?'

'Hawaii'

'Hawaii who?'

'Fine thanks, what about you?'

28

Knock Knock

'Who's there?'

'A pile up'

'A pile up who?'

'Yuk! *Suppose I'll have to clean it up, then.'*

29

Knock Knock

'Who's there?'

'Cash'

'Cash who?

'No thanks, I'm *allergic to nuts.'*

30

Knock Knock

'Who's there?'

'The *doorbell repair man!'*

Chapter Boom-Boommery

What have we learned this chapter? We can take you through the medium of a knock knock joke.

Knock Knock

Who's There

Jackson

Jackson Who?

Jacks on you, mate!

Final Words

And so, we reach the end. You have just read the best 400 or so jokes ever written. Somebody had to.

Thank you for doing this, and I will end with an apology. Sorry for the jokes that got away, the ones that didn't quite make it into this collection. Jokes such as:

A comment on society: Crime in multi-story parking lots. **Wrong on so *many different levels.***

Personal enlightenment: This is about me, George Smith. I have a secret. When I was a little younger I felt like a man trapped inside a woman's body. **Fortunately, it passed *after I was born.***

Family life: I always take my kid out at 12.59. **I like the *one to one time.*** It's probably because I was raised as an only child, which *really annoyed my sister.*

Society: A definition of working class. **When your TV is *bigger than your bookcase.***

Health: Life is like a box of chocolates. **It doesn't last long *if you're fat.***

And, finally…my wife told me recently that, 'Sex is better on holiday.' *I really didn't appreciate that postcard.*

Thanks again for taking the time to download this book!

If you enjoyed this book, please take the time to leave me a review on Amazon. I appreciate your honest feedback, and it really helps me to continue producing high quality books.

89275949R00083

Made in the USA
Lexington, KY
25 May 2018